# INSIDE OF HER

## JAMICKA LAKEYA

# DEDICATION

*All my beautiful Queens, my sisters, this one is just for you. We are all in this together. I really hope you enjoy it and this helps a little. I hope that I was able to bring some of the topics that you all gave me to life. Thank you, and I love you.*

# CONTENTS

# ACKNOWLEDGMENTS

Thank you for taking the time to purchase my baby. Thank you for giving her a chance. Thank you for supporting me and my work.

To all the women who gave me an insight into their life
To all the women who weren't afraid to let me in
To all the women who wanted to speak their truth
To all the women who wanted to be heard
To all the women who wanted a little more
To all women….
Thank you.

Special thank you to Alicia Mckie, Angel Moss, Kaneisha Lee, Naomi Washington, and Allison Denise.

# INTRODUCTION

*Inside Of Her* is an insight on women from women. *Inside Of Her* is the heart of a woman's desirable, intricate, resilient mind. It is the words of women, glistening and sliding down a women's body in the form of poetry. She is a collection of poems about the female's perspective and the insight of and on women, misconceptions, life, love, friendships, battles, and so much more. It is her mind, body, soul, thoughts, and everything else you could possibly think of. So if you've ever wanted to know what goes on inside a woman's mind or if you've ever just wanted a little insight on women, spread this book open and get to reading. I promise that you won't be disappointed. Sit back, relax, and allow yourself to get lost inside of a woman's thoughts and mind. And explore the inside of her.

# INSIDE OF HER

~

## To My Queens

To my queens, my sisters, my women
You are strong, beautiful, and intelligent.
Your gorgeous brown skin makes it hard for people not to give
you compliments.
Carry yourself with so much grace and poise.
Make a lot of noise without making a lot of noise.
Your fashion sense, the way you can style your hair is all one
of a kind.
You're like a unicorn, a mermaid, a majestic being that can't
be defined.
You are God's amazing creation, a wonderful addition to
anything.
My sister, you are a queen, now go and wear your crown
proudly.

**Fragments of Life**

Peace, joy, love, abundance, and happiness.
Wisdom, knowledge, blessings, and divine bliss.
Freedom, forgiveness, growth, and grace.
Meditation, manifestation, prayer, praise.
Hope, favor, mercy, and increase.
Healing, restoration, clarity, and stability.
Gratitude, health, affirmations, and perseverance.
Wealth, success, assets, and abundance.

## One In The Same

All my women, I just want you to know that I'm proud of you.
You all are obtaining multiple degrees, starting your own
businesses, and becoming head of corporations too.
Some of yall are raising a family and running your household
while taking care of you.
Wife, mother, business-woman, entrepreneur, doctor, nurse, or
whatever the title you hold true.
You are doing the damn thing, and I just want you to know
I'm proud and appreciate you.
With everything going on in this world, don't lose yourself,
and don't forget who you are.
Remember to always keep you and your peace a priority
because that's the hardest part.
Continue to speak up and let your voice be heard.
Fight for what you believe in and go get what you deserve.
Let your presence be felt and let yourself be known.
Because just being a woman is hard enough on its' own.

## Women Empowerment

As women, we should be rooting for each other instead of
bringing the next one down.
And I can understand friendly competition, but we should
never tilt our sisters' crown.
You don't have to dim her light to make yours shine.
What's for you will always be for you, and when it's your time,
it's your time.
Support your sister, cheer her on, uplift her, and show her
love.
Because this world is already putting her through more than
enough.
Tearing her down won't make you win or make things better
for you.
So treat her the same as you would want any other woman to
boost and support you.
Boost each other's ego, complement each other, and build
each other up.
Because carrying the world on our shoulders and back is
tough and already enough.
Strong women can be trusted; they lift each other and
celebrate one another.
They stick together because we know that we are stronger
together and should not break each other.
There is enough available out here for all of us to make it
and win.
So queens stick together, be powerful, and help each
other win.

## Let's Talk About Sex

They say I shouldn't talk about my sexual experiences or my
sex life.
I'm told there's no need for me to be vocal about sex and the
things that I like.
I shouldn't over-share because I may be considered a whore or
slut.
And it's just not lady-like, and "good girls" just don't talk
about it.
I'm told to play coy and leave some for people's imagination.
My sex and sex life is valuable, gorgeous but should also be
kept private.
It's frowned upon when a woman is too sexual publicly.
And to some, it's just plain trashy.
But, I shouldn't have to shy away from the topic or subject.
Because every day, I'm sexualized, and my body is looked at
and googled over as sexual imagery.
As women, we should be able to talk about our sexual
encounters.
I should be able to talk about what I want and what I deserve.
I should not be ashamed, judged, or feel uncomfortable to
share the feelings or joy of sex with my friends.
We women should be able to make up our own minds when it
comes to the topic at hand whether we love it or not.
It shouldn't be just a taboo topic; it's normal, life, and should
be accepted.
Sex, sexual activity, pleasure, foreplay, orgasms, should not just
be a topic that is only open, accepted, and for men to talk
about.
We, women, need to talk about it.
All parts of it.

## Because I'm A Woman

So because I'm a woman, I shouldn't have a voice.
I should stay in my place and stand behind a man.
Everyone else should make decisions for me, about me, and concerning me.
So because I'm a woman, I should only worry about being a mother or a wife.
I should take three steps behind.
And I should know my role and stay in my place.
So because I'm a woman, I shouldn't have a lead role and shouldn't be qualified for the same job as a man.
I should take and play the role of a homemaker and only do things around the house.
Follow someone else's order and make them look good.
So because I'm a woman, I can't have too much ambition or be too successful.
I need to lay low and play coy because I don't want to threaten the man or upstage him.
Because if I do too much, I'll be considered manly or trying to take the role of a man.
So because I'm a woman...
No...because I AM A WOMAN I'M POWERFUL, I'M A BOSS, I'M A QUEEN. AND I AM IN CONTROL!

## Do You

It's ok to not want to be a mother and to not want kids.
Everyone's life and story aren't the same so let them live their
life as is.
It's ok to not want to be an entrepreneur and work for
yourself.
Some people would rather move up in the business and
corporate world and focus on a different type of wealth.
It's ok if you prefer to stay single and don't want the "married
life."
You don't have to live that lifestyle of being someone's
husband or wife.
It's ok if you want to be a stay at home parent and focus on
the tasks at hand.
Take care and focus on your family, your home, and being an
amazing stay at home parent.
It's ok if you want to live a fairytale life and do everything that
you've dreamed.
It's your life to live so please do what makes you happy by any
means.
Don't let society or people rush or push you into something
that's not for you.
Don't let anything hold you back or hinder your from doing
what you want to do.
It's ok to move slowly and at move at your own pace.
It's ok to be different and want things not like the rest, take
your time; this life is not a race.

## Stuck

Sometimes I feel like I'm not doing enough
Like I'm not where I should be in life and that I'm just stuck.
I feel as if I'm behind or should have accomplished a lot more
than what I have.
Like I'm not taking advantage of life, not living enough, or
even doing the half.
Like I should be happily married by now or even have a
couple of kids.
Like I should be at the top of a company, an entrepreneur, or
managing some type of business.
I should be taking trips around the world, having spa days, or
just taking advantage of caring for myself.
Plentiful in love, relationships, success, and wealth.
Maybe I should be further along in life and be more successful
than I am.
Have more money saved, invested in stock, invest in real
estate, have an amazing business plan.
Do a little more and be a little more so I won't feel stuck and
stagnant.
Take the next step, reinvent me, don't compare my journey to
someone else's, or let society make me feel like I'm not valid or
advancing.

**Achieve**

Don't take no for an answer if it's stopping you from pursuing
your dreams.
Be bold, take risks, and do what you want and believe.
Trust in yourself, believe in your power, and dig deep inside
of you.
Exceed your own expectations, build your own kingdom, and
do what makes you proud of you.

Never expect people to
do for you what you
do for them because if
you do, you'll be a fool
and disappointed too.

*Jamicka*

If you're looking for the old me, you won't find her; she has grown too much and gone too far to come back.

*Jamicka*

## Labels

I'm sick and tired of you trying to put a label on me.
Angry, feisty, bougie, stuck up, or whatever you think of me.
Before you try to label and critique me, take a look at yourself.
Because you shouldn't throw rocks from inside a glasshouse,
especially if you're not perfect yourself.

You are not meant to
blend in, be different, be
you, embrace it; it's ok.
Don't fall into the trap
that society had made and
put on us...
STAND OUT!

*Jamicka*

**The Way I Dress**

So because I'm dressed a certain type of way, it gives you the
right to talk to me how you please?
But what if I judged you based on the way you looked and
dressed and called you everything less than a king?
It doesn't matter what I wear, I'm still a woman, and you
should respect that.
Just like you wear your pants to your knees, baggy or tight
clothes, or your hat turned to the back,
Form-fitting clothes, a dress, a suit, or whatever I wear, it
doesn't define me.
So don't use that as an excuse or reason to come at me
incorrectly.
I'm not a bitch, a hoe, a slut, a tramp, or any of those names.
So think twice before disrespecting me because if I judged you
by the way that you dress, then we would be one and the
same.

Everyone
is entitled to their
opinion, but I could
care less about yours.

*Jamicka*

## Our Physical

People always have an opinion or say so when it comes to a
woman.
An opinion about the way our bodies look, even to the way
that we should or shouldn't dress.
They tell us that makeup is too much but can't handle natural
as if natural is not enough.
That we should do without weave and embrace our natural
hair but like more of the straight and "tamed look."
Or that we should work out to be what they call "slim thick"
because that's what they like and our bodies would look better
that way.
Well…I'm here to tell you; it's not our purpose to please you
or anybody else for that matter.
What we choose to do with us is simply that.
This is our body and our choice… and we don't need your
criticism, input, or validation.

Be who you want to be; don't let people define or label you!

*Jamicka*

## Stronger Than A Man

As women, when we get hurt, we're just supposed to move on
and learn how to love again.
We often get mistreated, cheated on, heartbroken, and
expected not to have a guard up with the next man.
We "can't" just sulk in our heartbreak and decide to give up
on love.
Or be "mad at the world" or "play the field" until we feel like
we've played around enough.
We're supposed to just take it as a lesson learned and apply
that lesson to the next.
Give the next man a fair shot and forget about our past and
just put all the pain and turmoil to rest.
Don't make it too hard for the next man to get to know us or
break down the walls we've managed to put up.
Because there is only so much a man can put up with before
he decides enough is enough.
But somehow, things change when all this happens to a man.
They can walk around mad at the world and make it hard for
a woman to get close to them again.
Men walk around and act like women don't get hurt more
often than not.
Like it's the end of the world when it happens to them, and
they end up so distraught.
Instead of healing themselves and opening up so that they
may be able to love again.
They decide that almost every woman is the same, and for
now, it's no point putting their all into a relationship again.
Men's lives turn upside down when one woman does them
wrong.
Then they decide to never let another woman in, harbor pain
and string every other woman along.

They give up on love, give up on having a real relationship,
and just make things all about sex.
Because they've been left, mistreated, cheated on, done wrong,
and now everyone woman is just like his ex.
Because they'd rather not deal with the hurt and pain again,
they just take that L and "charge it to the game."
And decide never will I make that mistake again, or will I ever
be the same.
Man or woman, male or female, we both have been through a
significant amount of pain.
But things shouldn't be different for either gender when it
comes to opening up and loving again.
So men, when you get your heartbroken, trust me, we women
understand.
But that doesn't mean shut the entire world out and be a dog
and never love or trust a woman again.

## Melanin Misconceptions

Dark skin vs. light skin, colorism, melanin misconceptions
Society has us going crazy over a certain type of skin...fair
skin, light skin, brown skin, dark skin,
But no skin is more beautiful than the next skin, well at least
that's what most of us try to tell ourselves.
Well, in actuality, society has shown us that if you're light skin,
you're more attractive, you're quicker to grasp attention or
quicker to get the job.
Society has made us think that if you're light skin, you're
prettier than someone who is of a darker complexion.
We all have experienced some type of hate when it comes to
our skin.
For example...
You're pretty for a dark-skinned girl.
Dark skinned women are too manly.
Those light skin people act bougie and stuck up.
Light skin women are too sensitive.
She's too light; she is not black.
You're so dark; you're purple.
She's too dark for that hair color, she's too dark for that color,
and dark-skinned people shouldn't wear that.
She's so light I can see right through her.
Light skin people think they're entitled just because they're
light skin.
And I'm pretty sure all these sound too familiar.
And you've probably heard more or worse.
But remember your black is beautiful, your skin is beautiful.
No matter your skin, love your skin.
Over here, we don't have time for colorism or melanin
misconceptions.

**66**

Who you are, your identity, and your worth doesn't come from the validation of other people or what people think of you. Your identity comes from the Lord and lies in that first. Be true to you.

*Jamicka*

**Your Impression**

Wait….weight

Weight seems to be a touchy subject, but it takes a toll on the best of us.

We get criticized for being too skinny, or we're told that we're too big.

Often times we're told we need to gain weight because we're too small.

Or we need to lose weight because we've gotten too big.

If I wear something flirty and form-fitting or even showing a little skin, I'm told I need to cover up because I'm too fat to be wearing clothes like that.

But if I'm athletic or "slim thick," I'm told to show off my figure more and wear more form-fitting clothes or just wear less.

And if I'm too skinny, I'm told that I need to eat more and maybe even consider surgery.

It's ok for a size 4 to be proud and flaunt her body, but a size 12 cannot?

It all seems to be like a double standard.

Little do you know; I've tried to lose weight, I've taken the pills, tried the quick schemes, and even starved myself.

I've also eaten more than not, I've taken the supplements, and I've done the workouts.

And before you think about greeting me with, "you're so skinny" or "you've gained some weight, please think again.

You let society's definition of beautiful and the "ideal weight" get you all mixed up.

Because what you don't know and understand is I could care less what you think about my weight.

I know my weight doesn't define me, and no matter what, I know I'm beautiful and proud of what I have.

## Angry Black Woman

So because I voice my opinion and speak up for myself, I'm an
angry black woman.
Because I refuse to let you treat me any kind of way, I have an
attitude.
Because I don't allow you to manhandle me and talk to me
any kind of way, I'm considered disrespectful.
Because I bite back and don't let you get away with things, I'm
confrontational.
Because I don't partake in certain festivities and tell you my
business, I'm sneaky and not a good person.
Because I refuse to be fake with you and tell it like it is, I'm
rude.
So because I refuse to bow down, "play nice," and be
something I'm not, I'm an angry black woman.

"

You have to believe in
yourself, celebrate yourself,
be proud of you, and pat
yourself on the back. Don't
wait for others to
celebrate you.

*Jamicka*

She was the hidden jewel
that they didn't take the
time to know to know or
find.

*Jamicka*

## She Never

She never said anything because she was too embarrassed and
ashamed.
She even thought that part of it could have been her own
fault.
She blamed herself for it so many times and for it even
happening the way that it did.
She didn't think that people would believe her if she would
have said something anyway.
She didn't want people to judge her, pity her, or look at her
differently.
Maybe if she had thought more clearly or made another
choice, it wouldn't have happened.
Maybe if she hadn't been so naive, she could have saved
herself some trauma and pain.
Maybe if she hadn't worn those types of clothes, she wouldn't
have enticed him.
Maybe she should have never gone there because that
probably gave the wrong sign.
Maybe just maybe.
She never thought it could or would happen to her.
She never spoke up because she was afraid.
She never spoke up because she was clueless and didn't know.
She never spoke up because people would judge her and tell
her she's lying because she waited so long to speak up.
She never spoke up because she didn't know how to.
She never spoke up.
Unfortunately, it's something she'll never forget and have to
live with forever.
But it happened to her....
Sexual Assault.

Self-care
is more important than you
think; learn to take care of
you first.

*Jamicka*

In every moment in your life, there is a woman in your life.
From the good to the bad, through the troubles and the strife.
From the time you arrived until you depart.
She is there from beginning to end, from finish to start.
Mother, sister, friend, girlfriend, wife, or whatever role she plays.
She is the one who is always there with you, and even during the hard times, she stays.
She is constant, consistent, and one that you'll always need.
She is different; there is no other like her; she is a different breed.
But even when *she* leaves, another comes and replaces her.
Because you need a WOMAN in your life, and nothing can be a substitute for her.

**Men Need**

Ladies, a lot of times, we like to blame it all on the men.
But sometimes we can be the cause of making the
relationship/friendship come to an end.
We put all this pressure on a man to be the perfect man and
be everything we may need.
While missing the simple things and forgetting about the
things he may want or need.
Sex is one vital component and more important than not.
And if that need isn't met or we can't satisfy him, then nine
times out of ten, the relationship can be shot.
Yes, sex is important, but men also need intimacy too.
Because just as we do, a man wants to be appreciated too.
We can be "toxic," compare him to others or try to fix him up.
Which makes him feel less than or like he isn't enough.
We tend to not trust him, accuse him of lying and cheating
amongst many other things.
While not motivating him, supporting him, or uplifting him,
and everything else in between.
Just as he has your back, he needs you to have his.
And to do little things for him, cater to him sometimes and
show and tell him why he's important.
Feed him, mentally, intellectually, spiritually, and emotionally.
Stroke his ego, build him up, and keep the relationship lively.
Apologize, take ownership, and turn things around for the
better.
Because it's not always the man, sometimes it's us, and we're
the reason why he decided to leave, go off, and do better.

**For The Record**

Wine, beer, liquor, weed
Whatever it is to take the pain away and make the void leave.
Late nights out, bars, clubs, partying and roaming the town
Avoiding being by myself, getting to know me, and constantly having someone around.
Surrounding myself with people that I know are no good for me.
"Friends" that I can't even have a deep conversation with, friends that only want to get lit, turn up, and drink.
Plundering through apps like Tinder, Bumble, and Hinge to find the "perfect man."
To show me a good time, to hit the right spots, and take some time off my hands.
Running away from my problems, thoughts, mind, and the fact that without it, I'm lonely.
So I'm doing whatever I can so I don't have to face the fact that it's just me.
The fact that I'm drowning and doing whatever I can to not feel what I feel and escape this terrible reality.

**Missing Piece**

"

Until you learn to love
yourself and put yourself
first, there is no amount of
work a man can do to take
away the hurt.

*Jamicka*

Instead of trying to lay with me... how about you pray with me.
Grow, converse, build, and learn how to do this crazy thing called life with me.

*Jamicka*

Her book was highly intricate, too elaborate, so he would never get to open her.

*Jamicka*

"

Until
you learn to love yourself
and put yourself first, there
is no amount of work a
man can do to take away
that hurt.

*Jamicka*

Be upfront and tell me what you want from me.
Sex, money, friendship, a relationship, or just someone to keep you busy.
I'd respect you more if you would tell me and let me know.
Then it would be my decision to stay or let you go.
Don't lead me on, tell me what I want to hear, or try to waste my time.
Because to be honest, with or without you in my life, I'll be just fine.

**Tell Me What You Want**

##

"

The most beautiful part of
her, he wasn't delicate
enough to touch.

*Jamicka*

Can you stimulate the inside of me?
Feel me up and take care of my entire body
Hit all the right spots and penetrate my mind
Open me up, seduce me with your charm and send shivers
down my spine
Touch every inch of me, my heart, my mind, and my soul
Undress my thoughts and my ideas without fully being
exposed
Use your mind to leave your marks and thoughts all over me
Pleasing my heart, mind, and soul…making me weak to my
knees
No sex involved right now, just mental penetration
Thoughts, chakras, minds, connecting just mental stimulation.

**Stimulation**

Do you know how to touch me without touching me?
How to keep me stimulated intellectually?
How to help me open up emotionally so I can share my
darkest desires with you confidently?
How about spiritually?
Am I able to share with you and talk to you about morals,
values, and even spiritual beliefs?
Do you know how to make love to me mentally?
How to caress my thought process and go deep inside my
creativity?
How to connect with my mind and give me that ultimate
release that I need?
How to teach me, open up to me, and explore me fully?
Do you know how to turn me on without pleasing me
sexually?
Because you see, sex is easy, and I need more to arouse and
stimulate me.

**How To**

Even when I know I shouldn't, I still continue to do so.
Caught up in the moment, the vibe, the what if, and I can't
seem to let go.
From the moment I decided to say yes and give you a try.
I knew that I would be hooked, dependent, and addicted to
the high.
You filled my body with peace and happiness and even kept
me sane.
From the moment I took a whiff and inhaled, I knew that
things would never be the same.
When I had you around, I was a completely different me.
I was on cloud nine, head in the clouds, less stressed, and
carefree.
I knew something was wrong when I became too dependent
on you.
When I needed you around for simple things, to go to sleep, or
just to make it through.
I knew you were toxic and would cause me more harm
than not.
But I was addicted to the feeling, the high, the ecstasy, and the
amazing feelings you brought.
It wasn't until I started to lose sight of me and who I was
before I was introduced to you,
That I knew, I could no longer do this, and it would be best
for me to be without you.

**Addicted**

66

Let me know my title in your life so I can play the part I need to because there is no way in hell I'm going to be doing the things that a partner of wife would do.

*Jamicka*

I loved you until….


I loved you more than you loved yourself
I loved you until I couldn't love anymore
I loved you until I didn't know how to love anymore
I loved you until I had no more love to give
I loved you until it hurt me
I loved you even after you hurt me
But it's funny how things change….
I taught you how to be a better person
I taught you how to be a better man
I taught you how to love
I even taught you how to treat a woman….too bad that woman wasn't me.
I taught you how to do ALL the right things… for someone else!

**I Loved You Until**

If you didn't want to be with me, that's all you had to say,
Not string me along, waste my time, or try to run the game you play.
Calling me your associate but then wanting me to act like your girlfriend,
Wanting me to take care of you, drive to see you, and do everything a girlfriend would do but just as a friend.
Oh, let me rephrase that, not even a friend but just an associate,
One that lifts you up motivates you, sleeps with you, and gives you everything you want without the commitment.
Talking to me and texting me all day every day, but telling me you're so busy and you don't have the time,
Time to settle down, time for a relationship, time to commit to one female, time to make time.
But all the while stringing me along and making me feel like something that it's not
Just to occupy your time until you find the right one but just as an associate and not in that girlfriend or wife spot.

**Associate**

I think it's best if I just take a break from you.
Because I don't know how much longer I can be just friends with you.
I try to mask my feelings, tuck them away, or simply keep them hidden.
But sometimes I can't help myself because I've never met someone like you, someone so different.
You're funny, sweet, easy to talk to, a business and God-fearing men.
And sometimes I can't help but wonder if you'll ever be anything more than a friend.
You're always there for me and know things about me that most don't know.
And I can read you, know when something's wrong, and lend a hand without you even saying so.
When you ask for advice or a woman's point of view, I give it because that's what friends do.
I tell you to take a chance, go for it, go out with her, all the while wishing it was me that was with you.
I honestly thought I could just separate the two and just have you as my friend.
But the more we talk and are together, the thoughts and ideas play in my mind over and over again.
I hate for it to be like this, but its best right now if I just walk away.
Because I wouldn't do anything to jeopardize our friendship or relationship in any way.


**Friend-Zoned**

Dear _____,

I think you need to let her know that you were out here telling me and everyone else that you were single. Confess to her that you weren't faithful and were quick to go out and cheat on her. You started seeing someone behind her back and thought it would be a great secret to keep. Confess to her that you were out here, spending the majority of your time with me. Tell her how you told me you wanted nothing more than to be with me, how I was different, and no matter what, you'd always have an open heart for me. Man up and let her know how I was "so easy to talk to" and to be with and how you were so comfortable with me. How I was so different from anybody you had ever met, how I supported you like no ever had, and always had your back and your best interest at heart. Confess to her that you never wanted to let me go and always wanted me around. Tell her how you didn't want to lose me and only wanted to make me happy. Confess to her that it killed you to think about me or see me with someone else because you had to have me. Tell her the truth that it wasn't me because I'm nobody's secret and play second fiddle to none. Tell her I had no idea she was even in the picture because you're the one that lied. Tell her the truth. Tell her about me and see if she's ok with the secret you wanted to keep. If your girl only knew.....
But you better tell her before I do because had you us both out here looking like some fools. CONFESS!!!

**Confess**

If you can't love her the way she needs to be loved, then learn to let her go.
She is more than a token, a trophy, or a body just to be seen with you for show.
She deserves someone who will love her, inside and out.
A man who will build with her, break barriers with her, and show her what love is about.
Someone who is not afraid to be vulnerable and states how he feels.
A partner that knows about support, God, balance, change, love, peace, and what it means to be real.

**If You Can't**

He loved me so much that he showed it EVERY WAY
possible.
He loved me so much that he broke me down just to build me
back up.
He loved me so much that he showed it through his stern
powerful powerful stern tone of voice.
He loved me so much he left his prints and marks ALL over
my body.
He loved me so much he would call me every name but the
one I was given.
He loved me so much he wanted to keep me all to
himself.....trapped.
He loved me so much he kept me locked up, he controlled me,
and he beat me.
He loved me so much...

**He Loved Me**

See, I was beaten by your abusive words, cut by your thick
slick, sharp tongue, torn, ripped apart, and undressed by your
mesmerizing deceitful eyes…..
And here I find myself naked, covered with bruises, trapped,
trying to hide it all behind a disguise.

**Abused**

I'm the woman that they should have treated right and held on to... but by the time they realize it; it's too late.

*Jamicka*

I've been hurt numerous amounts of times, but I still love as if no pain exists.

*Jamicka*

**Him: You write and speak about pain a lot.**

*Me: I write and speak about it because I've experienced it a little too much, and I know it a little too well.*

I wish that I could explain to you the way that I feel.
But there are no words to describe what's going on in my mind, and I can't make it seem real.
I don't know what's going on, and I really don't know what's wrong.
Everything is ok, but it's not ok, and I've been feeling like this for way too long.
My thoughts are all over the place, and my emotions are on edge.
I could be happy at one moment or drop down and cry at the next.
My mind goes in overdrive; I panic, get nervous and find a lot of things more difficult than not.
I'm happy on the outside, but sometimes the battles inside myself are more than I can handle and tear me apart.
I wish I could tell and explain to you what's really going on, but the only words I can find are I'm fine.
Because in the end, you won't really understand, you'll start to judge me, tell me it's my fault, or it's all in my mind.

**No Words**

I used to be afraid to lose someone or let a relationship go.
I became co-dependent and did what I could to make sure the relationship would and could grow.
But after a while, I started not to care because of the one-sided friendships/relationships I couldn't do anymore.
It put a strain on me because it felt as if I was the only one putting forth the effort.
Continuously there for everyone else and supporting everyone but me.
But when it came to them, I was their number one fan, supporting, clapping, and being there with advice happily.
Yeah, letting go may be time and years possibly wasted, but it's better to let go now.
Especially when things aren't getting better, and everything is and seems to be going south.
I can't continue to check on someone, support someone, root for someone, and be all in for someone who doesn't do the same.
Because while they're living their life and reaping the benefits, I'm the one second-guessing everything.
Make room for someone who values you and respects the relationship and puts forth the same effort as you do.

**Reciprocation**

So when I start treating you like you treat me, then we have a problem.
But everything was all good when you were wasting my time, playing around, running from our problems, and not trying to solve them.
And to be honest, the only person you have to blame is you.
Because if you had been real and upfront in the beginning, all of this could have been avoided too.
So now that I've stopped replying back and I'm unbothered, you want to show that you care.
You want to act like it's all my fault and how I'm moving now is unfair.
See, you created the path, and I just followed the way,
And I decided to turn things around on you and play the same games you play.

**Same Treatment**

It's ok for you, but a problem for me.

See, you're not practicing what you preach, and that's hypocrisy and, in some cases, a double standard mentality.

You can talk to and have multiple women and even choose to sleep around,

But the minute I even decide to give more than one man my time, I'm considered a whore and the talk of the town.

You can make dirty jokes, freely talk about sex, make derogatory comments about women, and what it would be.

But if I do anything to that nature, it's frowned upon, and I'm told that's not how a lady should be, and I should be discreet.

You can mistreat me, cheat on me, not communicate, and still expect me to stay.

But let me turn the tables on you, do the same to you, and then we have a problem, and it's not ok.

You can do and dish out all this mess but can't take it back, but if you do it, it's fine.

Because you're a man, it's ok, but since I'm a woman, it's not acceptable, and I need to stay in line.

**Double Standards**

So what if I decided to reverse the roles on you?
Treat you like you treated me and put you through all the hell
you put me through.
Feed you all kinds of lies and tell you everything you want to
hear.
Spend time with you, treat you right, then up and disappear.
Treat you like you're the only one, while I'm out here
doing me.
Make you feel so happy when I'm only using you for my
needs.
Ignore your messages and ignore your phone calls.
Don't care about your feelings, your emotions, and make you
feel so small.
Lead you on, give you false hope, and make you think it's
something that it's not.
Leave you alone, find someone else, then come back to you
when that other thing isn't working out how I thought.
Reel you back in just to get you where I want you, only to end
up breaking your heart.
But it'll be cool because we were never in a relationship, and I
never wanted that part.
So, what would you do if I decided to reverse the roles
on you?

**Reverse**

Just when I started to rethink some things and actually started liking you.
When I thought, just give it a chance, you never know what this may lead to.
I thought to myself, talk to God, and see what he has to say.
Ask him if this is the man for you and if he is in your life to stay.
He told me yes, he is an amazing man, but he'll be no more than another lesson.
He's not meant to be your lover, your husband, so try not to get too invested.

**Another Lesson**

You were my comfort zone, my peace, me escape, my happy place.
You were that one thing that I could depend on to take all the stress and pain away.
You were my security, my safe haven, my home away from home.
You were that one thing that I could run to when everything was going wrong
You were my light, my sweet dream, the lyrics to my favorite love song.
You were that one thing that I knew that I could always depend on.
You were my strength, my joy, my pain reliever, my all of the above.
You were that one thing that I thought I would always love.
You were my happiness, my laughter, the warm embrace of a hug.
You were that one thing that I thought I would never get enough of.

**You Were**

"

You ask me if I love you,
and I tell you that I do but
sometimes love isn't enough
to get us through all the
hurt, issues, and pain we've
been through.

*Jamicka*

If I knew then what I know now, maybe I would have done
things a little differently.
I would have stayed a little longer.
I would have smiled a little harder.
I would have laughed a little louder.
I would have loved a little stronger.
I would have held on a little tighter.
I would have never let go.

**If I Only Knew**

66

When I learned to let you go
completely is when I
realized I only loved the
thought of us and the
potential of you...what we
could have been.

*Jamicka*

Miss me when I'm gone....
So now that I'm gone, you miss me and want me back.
You see me glowing, living my best life, and getting everything back on track.
See, you left, and I realized that was the best thing that could have happened to me.
But it sucks for you because I guess she wasn't all that you thought she was going to be.
Now that she's gone and you have no one by your side,
It's, "I'm sorry, I miss you, and I'll do whatever I can and even put my pride to the side."
See, you had a good thing, and you messed around and let it go.
All for something that looked good on the outside but like I told you before, everything that glitters isn't gold.
So now it's, "I love you, I want you back, and everything I say is sincere."
But it's too late because you see everything you could have imagined and asked for; it was all right here.

**You Realized**

I just wrote this poem to tell you that this time is the last time.
The last time I put my trust in you, and the last time I let you
put me through what you put me through.
The last time I take you back and the last time I put up with
your slack.
The last time I believe your lies and the last time l let you
make me cry.
The last time I return your calls and the last time I give you
my all.
The last time I even consider, the last time I allow you to make
me bitter.
The last time I even care about you, the last time I want
ANYTHING to do with you.

**The Last Time**

"

That one piece of her that you held on to, to always be able to string her along... Well, she FINALLY decided to cut it and release that piece that she was attached to for far too long.

*Jamicka*

66

The day I found peace
is the day I left you.

*Jamicka*

Don't hold it in any longer,
scream, write about it, talk
about it, escape it.
Don't let it hold you hostage
any longer.
Breathe...Inhale,
exhale, let it go.

*Jamicka*

I know that you've been hurt, failed, let down, mistreated, and judged, but don't allow that or someone to make you miss out on what God and life have for you. It's ok to start over, open up, and tear down some of the walls you've built. Because what's for you can be that next step you're afraid to take and/or right behind those walls, you won't let down. You have to be willing and can't be afraid to take that next leap.

~

I've done so much for the wrong guy; I can't wait to see what I'll do for the right man.

*Jamicka*

**Are You Ready?**

I'll love you how you've always wanted and needed to be
loved.
I'll make sure that with me, you'll get more than enough.
I'll respond to you and treat you like no one has ever have.
Give you things you didn't know you wanted and experiences
you've never had.
Ease your mind so that you will feel safe and secure with me.
Make it easy for you to open up and be comfortable with
venting to me.
Have your back, build you up, support you like your woman
should.
Play around and joke with you, love you in your love language,
and always make sure you're good.
I know it'll take time, and I'll hold nothing against you.
Because I know it's hard when you've been through the mud,
and it's time to try something new.
And just like you've been hurt, I've been hurt too.
But I promise with me you don't have to worry and can let
your guard down because I'll do anything for you.
I'm not her; and I promise not to treat you like your last.
I know what it's like to be done wrong and taken for granted,
but with me, we'll get over your past, and you don't have to
worry about that.

## Ingredients

Your rich milk chocolate gave me a sugar high I can't explain.
I'm drunk from your words and your intoxicating scent has
me going insane.
Your silky smooth skin is like satin and has me completely
drawn to you.
Your deep raspy voice lingers in my mind, and I can't help but
think of you.
Your strong muscular physique is like a work of art, and I
can't help but stare.
Your beautiful bright smile is so captivating; no one can
compare.
Your glistening mahogany eyes make me melt when I look
at you.
When it comes to you, I'm just so drawn, mesmerized, and
completely in love with all of you.

## Dear Black Kings

When the world is up against you, just know that I have your
back,
And you don't have to worry about anything because I'll pick
up whatever you lack.
In a society where you're degraded, falsely accused, and
always seem to be in the wrong,
Just know I'll be there with you and for you and making sure
you're mentally and physically strong.
When you feel like you've lost hope, down and out, and can't
take it anymore,
You'll find me right beside you, praying, pushing you,
motivating you, and letting you know that you're worth so
much more.
If you're going through something or need to talk, just know
that that doesn't make you any less of a man,
And I'll be whatever you need that listening ear, therapist,
shoulder to cry on, and best friend.
And when you feel like you need help, you don't even have to
ask because you know that I got you,
Because I support you, see what you do, and I know your
value.
Because I know you're a king, you're important, and you're
destined for greatness,
I'll always be beside you, uplifting you, pushing you, and
letting you know and making sure that there's a beat that you
don't miss.

**Vibe**

Can I lie on your chest while I listen to your heartbeat?
Have a meaningful conversation while our breaths and
breathing sync?
Do absolutely nothing but enjoy each other's presence.
Explore each other like we never have and in a much deeper
sense.

**Cater To You**

All the things you do for me, how about I do something nice
for you.
Sit down and relax, because tonight, I'm going to take care
of you.
Do all the things you like because I'm about to cater to you.
Tell me all about your day while you find something
comfortable to change into.
Cook your favorite meal just the way you like it.
Run your bath water and have your favorite liquor to go
beside it.
Massage your body so you can unwind and relax.
Let you play your favorite games while you lay on my lap.
Set the tone and mood before we go to bed, let you have your
way, and I'll show you why I'm the best you ever had.

## Quality Time

Play in my hair while I lie in your arms.
Pull me close and intoxicate me with your charm.
Watch my favorite movies with me, and let me read your
favorite books to you.
Gaze at me while I do my makeup and tell me the natural
look is your favorite look.
Dance with me around the house while we listen to music and
do chores.
Have a pillow fight before bed, and hold me tightly afterward.
Kiss me on my forehead before you go to leave.
Tell me you love me and promise you'll always come back to
me safely.

## Celibacy

This has nothing to do with the next person but a
commitment that she made to herself.
To not give another man any part of her that he wouldn't
cherish and love likes he loves himself.
A spiritual journey for her to focus, grow closer with God,
reevaluate, love, and cherish every part of her.
Because she knows that sex complicates things and makes
things worse, and it's more than just sex to her.
Her mind and body is a masterpiece, a work of art, and
should be treated with respect.
And she'd rather you get to know her, love her for her before
she commits to having sex.
To her, there's more to a relationship, and she'd rather know
and experience him on a deeper level instead.
Connect with him spiritually, grow with him, and build,
instead of first jumping in bed.
See, she believes in soul ties and will not be tied up with
another soul or just any man again.
Especially one that isn't willing to make her a wife and not
capable of being a husband.
The right man will be sent from God and will be willing to
wait for her.
Because he knows how valuable she is, he understands it's
more to her body, and he knows her worth.
So she'll do what's best for her, no matter what anyone has to
say because this is a commitment she made to herself and
God, and she wouldn't have it any other way.

## Angel Divine

For months I carried you inside of me
I was excited from the time I found out to the time I heard
your first heartbeat.
I loved you tremendously even before I met you, my precious
child, my baby.
My connection with you grew by the second, and I was in love
deeply.
With every kick, nudge, and movement you made
Was a blessing and I was so blessed to have you because, for
you, I had prayed.

But as time went on, things started to turn and started to
drastically change
I didn't feel those flutters, those movements, and your
heartbeat seemed to fade.
The same beautiful life that was growing inside of me,
Was unfortunately taken away and died inside of me.

A love so strong, a love like I've never met, I had to let go.
It tore me apart and broke my heart because I could no longer
see or feel you grow.
I would never get to hold my child in my arms or see them
laugh or hear them cry.
I couldn't even say hello before I had to say goodbye.

The pain I went through I honestly can't explain
But I just knew from then on out that life for me would never
be the same.
I am still blessed to have felt you and witness some amazing
parts
And even though you're not here physically, you'll always be
in my heart.

No matter what, I am still a mother, and my child is an angel divine
But God needed you more right now, and we'll be together in another lifetime.

## Do Not Disturb

I don't care to know about your problems or what you are going through.
I have issues of my own that I need to figure out and sort through.
I am not in a place where I can carry both your load and mine too.
I need space, to be alone, and to be selfish with my time.
To learn to say no, to take care of me, and learn to handle mine.
I am temporarily unplugged for personal development and self-care.
Leave me alone, do not disturb because, for the time being, I do not care.

66

Even when you think your
life is at a standstill and
everything is going wrong
or downhill, know that God
is working in the
background and for your
good.

*Jamicka*

## My Best Part

To the man that I met in my dreams, the tall chocolate
African king, the man that rescued me from defeat, the man
that came into my life and swept me off my feet, the man that
learned how to love every part of me, the man who treats me
like his everything…. that man, my man.
He's all I'll ever want and need, and he doesn't have to worry
about anything. No matter what, I'll always be at his side, no
questions asked, whatever he needs, imma always be down to
ride. He's no less of a king, and I treat him just as that. He
shows me I'm his queen, so of course, I'll always have his
back. He's sweet to my soul and healing to my heart. I
honestly couldn't ask for anyone better because he's my best
part.

**The Man For Me**

Thanks for being the man that I need you to be.
You've been patient, nurturing, supporting, loving, and more
than I could have asked for honestly.
When I look at you, I see my entire world in your eyes.
And it's finally clear, and I understand why I went through
what I went through with those other guys.
You saw the best in me, loved, and respected me as no other
man could.
You made sure that I was taken care of mentally and
spiritually and always made sure we were good.
You loved me for me, didn't try to change me, and accepted
my flaws and all.
Even though I tried my hardest not to let you in, you stayed
and broke down every wall.
Thank you for showing me that not every man is the same.
Thank you for making it easy for me to trust, love, open up,
and give my heart to someone again.

## A Beautiful Thing

That feeling that I felt when I first found out was every
emotion I could possibly think of.
I was afraid, nervous, overwhelmed, full of joy, doubtful, and
even overthinking if I would be enough.
My life would quickly change at the drop of a dime, and all I
could do was prepare myself.
Hold on tight and get ready for the ride because life no longer
would just be about myself.
I questioned if I was ready and could handle everything that
was about to come my way.
If I really knew what I was about to get myself into because
this type of commitment would be forever and a day.
I was fearful of what my family and friends would think or
have to say.
But I had to be quick to realize that this was my life and my
choice and going to be my responsibility anyway.
Life as I knew it was slowing down and speeding up for me all
at the same time.
But I was about to be a part of something so miraculous and
amazing, and it would change my entire life.
All I knew is I didn't want to fail, and I just wanted to be the
best that I could for myself and my family.
Because this beautiful thing was another life growing inside
of me.

## As A Mother

As A Mother
I will always put your needs before my own.
You will always be well fed and taken care of.
Even when I don't have it, you will.
I will always create a way for you.
Your hobbies, your dreams, your goals, I'll forever support
you.
But I'm also going to give you tough love and give you the
truth.
I'll comfort you, cover you, protect you, and will forever
provide.
When you need a safe haven, you can come to your mother
and confide.
When no one else seems to be there, I will.
I may get angry and get frustrated sometimes
And I'll even be wrong a few times too.
I'll always be understanding and forgiving.
Know that I will stand up for you so you know you can count
on me.
Even when I don't want to, I will stand back while you fight
your own battles.,
I will let you make your own decisions and your own choices
because I believe in you, and I trust you.
My prayers will always involve you.
I will love you, no matter what.
And I will always do the best that I can
As A Mother.

## Friendship

We've grown so much over the years and have gained and
have lost.
Attitudes have changed, personalities have changed, and
distance has gotten farther.
There have been disagreements, marriages, weddings,
children, and new beginnings.
As time quickly passed us by and things changed, so have we.
Some friendships are still here, and some have grown apart.
And that is perfectly fine because everyone is not meant to be
there with you forever.
They were with you during the time you needed that one
thing in your life.
Friendships change, people change, and that is perfectly ok.
You can meet someone tomorrow, and they can have better
intentions than someone you've known forever and a day.
It isn't about how long you've known someone or how much
y'all have been through.
But about someone who grows with you, loves you, supports
you, and values the friendship just as much as you do.

I'm not just a friend that wants to have fun and "turn up" with you. I'm the friend that wants to see you win, the friend that wants to see you grow and pursue your goals. I'm the friend that pushes and encourages you, the friend that wants to see you and help you reach your fullest potential. I'm the type of friend that loves you, prays over, with, and for you.

## My Person

Losing a best friend can hurt worse than losing someone you
were in a relationship with.
It honestly feels like a part of you has left, and you have no
one to share those special times and memories with and
confide in.
Your 2 am, your person, the one you were the most vulnerable
and transparent with.
Is no longer that part of your life, and the relationship you
once had is now tarnished.
What you knew before is no longer, and your world is now
turned upside down.
Because without them, there is a void that right now, no one
can fill, so you feel a sense of emptiness now.
Your right hand, your confidant, and the bond that yall once
shared.
Has taken a toll for the worst and the friendship that once was
may not ever be repaired.
The person you could be your complete self with...
The person you could cry, laugh, pray, and have the most fun
with.
It is no longer that, and it hurts like hell.
Because you never thought about what it would be like to lose
someone who loved and knew you so well.
Losing your best friend is something that can't be put into
words...
Because losing someone that knew all your secrets, knew you
better than you knew yourself is a feeling unheard.

## Friends

Thanks for the secrets you've kept, the advice, the laughs, all
the memories, for having my back, being completely honest
with me, supporting me, and loving me.
Thank you for being there for me when I couldn't be there for
myself.
Thank you for not leaving when it got hard and for being an
adult and talking about it.
Thank you for not judging me.
Thank you for praying for me, praying with me, and uplifting
me.
Thank you for touching my heart and accepting me as grow,
and as I am.
Thank you for being you.

## Welcome Back

I learned how to love me when no one else could.
I taught myself how to be there for me when no one would or
understood.
No one could control my happiness, and I learned that it
didn't come from the next person or a materialistic thing.
The decisions on my life, my destiny, and to be a peace were
all on me.
I had to change the way I think, the way I look at things, and
my perspective on life.
How to control my thoughts, think positive, and manifest what
I wanted in life.
I had to know how to speak life and claim what is mine.
To put it in the atmosphere, ask, see, and believe, and it'll all
come in due time.
No matter how broken I thought I was, I learned that I could
turn it all around.
That the power was within me, the way I spoke, and to
reframe my mind and not let anything tear me down.
I learned to be full, at peace, and fill my life with whatever I
wanted.
To live and experience joy, freedom, laughter, happiness, and
love by using *"The Secret"* to be fully my entire existence.

## Miss Independent

I was taught to get it on my own and not depend on anyone else.
To find a way to get it and make it with little to no help.
I had to do what I had to do in order for things to work out for me.
Learn to do for me; expect nothing from no one because nothing in this life is free.
I was taught to learn how to take the challenges that life gave me and turn them around for my good.
To be strong, have tough skin, and sometimes misunderstood.
There were things I had to give up and know in the end; it would be worth the sacrifice.
To make do with what I had and make something out of nothing so I will be alright.
I learned that by any means necessary, do what you have to do to make sure that you are good.
Let nothing stand in your way, or deter your focus, take care of yourself, and be true to who you should.
So don't take offense when I'm not so dependent on you.
Because I was taught to get it on my own and be self-sufficient and do what I need to do.

## She Has Arrived

She questioned a lot of things about her, and she was unsure
of who she was
She didn't know what made her happy, and she didn't know
what she liked to do for fun
She was unaware of how to love herself and what it meant to
have peace within
She lost herself trying to please other people and always
putting on a façade
She pretended to be something she wasn't to blend in with
everyone else and avoid confrontation
She let other people and their opinions control her and get the
best of her
She felt the need to always be surrounded by people to drown
out her thoughts, and because she was afraid to get to know
herself
She was lost, she was hurt, she was broken.
After life started to take a toll on her, she learned and...
She can no longer be that person anymore
She learned what it meant to love her
She learned she can say no without excuses or explanations
She freed herself from the fear, anxiety, and depression
She valued her time alone in prayer and meditation
She found peace; she found her voice
She found out who she was, and she never let go.
She fell in love with her.

**66**

Inside of her...

She is divine bliss. She is
divine light. She is love. She
is peace. She is abundance.
She is beautiful. She is
intelligent. She is worthy.
She is enough. She is
poetry.

*Jamicka*

## About the Author

Jamicka Lakeya is an author, poet, and speaker. She released her first book, "Behind Closed Doors" in 2018. Shortly after, she was a co-author of the poetry book P.O.E.T.I.C. Jamicka has been writing poetry on and off since she was in middle school. Poetry is an outlet, an escape, and a way of expressing herself. Her focus is primarily on God, the journeys of life, lessons, relationships, mistakes, strengths, and the ones closest to her.

She is from a small town by the name of New Ellenton in South Carolina. She has a Bachelor's degree in Business Administration, Healthcare Management from Lander University. She is a member of the renowned organization Alpha Kappa Alpha Sorority, Inc.

You can contact Jamicka Lakeya on
Instagram: JamickaLakeya
Facebook: https://www.facebook.com/lakeya.hankinson